Flamenco Hips
and
Red Mud Feet

Camino del Sol

A Latina and Latino Literary Series

FLAMENCO HIPS
AND
RED MUD FEET

DIXIE SALAZAR

THE UNIVERSITY OF ARIZONA PRESS ⟿ TUCSON

For Jon, who always inspires

The University of Arizona Press
© 2010 Dixie Salazar
All rights reserved

www.uapress.arizona.edu

Library of Congress Cataloging-in-Publication Data
appear on the last printed page of this book.

Publication of this book is made possible in part by the proceeds of a
permanent endowment created with the assistance of a Challenge Grant
from the National Endowment for the Humanities, a federal agency.

Manufactured in the United States of America on acid-free, archival-
quality paper processed chlorine free.

15   14   13   12   11   10   6   5   4   3   2   1

CONTENTS

PART I. INSIDE

PART II. OUTSIDE

PART I

INSIDE

HALF AND HALF

(DOUBLE SONNET)

She won't drink her milk

choked down half of it

and now the carton,

a waxed house, waits half

empty like herself

or half full of mother's

Southern Baptist grits

and the still unspilled secrets—

foreign as overheard Spanish

verbs like *metir* and *engañar*,

unknown to her now,

but later she'll learn

new ones like *negar*

and *herir*. She'll watch

her mother's face shine

wetly, turning pages

of the Bible, asking

what to do when he

comes home, half full of

bitter coffee dregs

and light from dead stars.

But both the Bible

and the house will whisper

nada . . . while the girl

wonders if the house

is half empty or

full of tears that bead on

wax as the house splits in two.

engañar: to deceive

herir: to wound

metir: to lie

negar: to deny

Subjunctive Mood

(with excerpts from a spanish grammar book)

Saint Anthony . . .

why didn't you find him?

My father, of course . . . lost

wandering in a private desert

with no horizon point;

he looked everywhere,

even inside—on the top shelf

and under the bottom rung—

still, it stayed lost . . .

Si lo hubiera perdido, hubiera dicho algo.

If he had lost it, he would have said something.

This type of sentence,

which expresses a past unreal condition,

implies that the "if" clause was not fulfilled.

Every four years

he threw another search party,

rotated the tires like globes

spun to another hollow promise

of cities paved with heirloom gold—

threw us into the wagon loaded

with fishbowls, meat grinders,

rubber thongs, hula hoops,

and tines of broken forks—

the invisible urn of bones

piled on top.

And he whistled

while the rest of us watched

villages shrink

in the rearview mirror

down to the size of a teardrop.

The subjunctive mood in Spanish

has four tenses:

present, past, present perfect,

past perfect . . .

que lo halle

I hope that he finds it

que lo hallará

I hoped he would find it

que lo haya hallado

que lo hubiera hallado

I hoped that he had found it.

Eyes on the horizon, he missed

a lot—my brother sitting on the bench

waiting for the score to dip so low

the coach would send him in—

my pink-rimmed glasses

stuffed between batting and springs

I dared St. Anthony to find—

Mother's glass eye probing the dark

corners of indiscretions.

Whereas the indicative mood

expresses fact or certainty,

the subjunctive mood expresses

uncertainty or doubt

in the mind of the speaker or writer

as to the absolute truth

of his statement . . . it is used

to state something even contrary to fact.

Now his eyes are milky—

turned to the blocked light

that is me entering

the room, his face full

of forgetting, like one

who enters a room pondering

what he has come to find.

St. Anthony, he never invoked you,

I know, but how could he, lost

in his own cracked hourglass?

Somewhere along the trail

he lost it—but it hung on

to him . . . St. Anthony, finder

of lost umbrellas, spectacles,

and cracked watch fobs, enter

the long lost song of the train

that laps the miles and disturbs

his dreams; St. Anthony, bring peace

to the hungry odometer

of his heart.

SPELLING IT OUT

Let there be no mistake

about this. It was wrong—

both the spelling and the

way it happened. We all

said no, but that meant nothing

to him—dead-set

on killing our history.

With a secret sleight-of-hand—

presto—we're Anglo Saxon

with a lot to explain

except for him—master-

forger of names—at the same time,

El Maestro correcting stacks

of Spanish spelling tests.

Shipwrecked now in fog of dementia,

he forgets his latest lie—denies

everything, just to be safe

lost in "Survivor" and reality shows

that blare and fill his days, pale

reminders of the reality he's always

managed to blur.

On his island, we spelled

it his way, and no one

voted him off. Denied

the right to vote, we sank

into the new name,

drowned survivors

with a box of soggy documents.

Full of questions, I turn down the sound.

Why did you change our name? Who

was the girl in the photo

with my eyes? Was she

my sister? Why did you deny?

Why did we move

again and again? I don't ask

these questions—too late

to change anything . . . Now

I watch him drift

in the backwash of TV light—unaware

that he's forged his own death

certificate—unaware

that now I'm spelling it right.

STOLEN NAMES

(DOUBLE-LINKED SONNETS DOUBLED)

A jury of my peers

hidden in the cornfields

whispered the name stolen

right from my mouth, traded

on the black market

for a small gold star

and Wizard of Oz lunchbox,

but that evidence will not be allowed

when crickets click in the dark

like toys imported from Japan,

accusing me of impersonating myself

and lying in a foreign tongue.

But I will refuse to take the stand,

pleading for a translator

or hiding in a dormer room

where rose thorns scar inside out.

Between earth and sky a sparrow

scolds—the sounds from its throat

melting back from tribes lost

from their own migration.

In the morning I'll find a fledgling

pummeled by the neighbor's cat.

I'll try to feed it back to the nest

to bridge the gap between air that buoys

and air that lets go.

The wobbly leaves will send back an echo

that sounds like my name, a mocking

half-cry perched between two worlds.

Swept in the blur of car lights,

a child disobeys and rolls down

the car window to gulp

darkness, to smell time shifting

and taste old fish bones in the wind.

She'll swallow the bitter vowels

of a lost name, and the gold star

she treasured will wobble

in the rearview mirror,

caught between the moving present

and the untranslatable past,

between a name she whispers

in the dark and the new one

winging over the playground.

And the sparrow that doesn't know

it's a sparrow sings on beyond

crossword puzzles and suicide notes,

Sid Vicious and Walt Whitman,

birthday cards and forged certificates,

beyond the darkness

of its own throat,

its song echoing across

Mississippi cotton fields

and centuries of docking boats,

old dialects, and new betrayals where

women in shawls curtsy to bow-tied men

with gold cuff links, stamping documents

with whatever name or spelling they desire.

No Wonder

there are nights

when the insomniac moon

stares me down, hooked

in the tintype faces of two grandmothers

from Memphis and Seville

facing off across the dresser scarf

embroidered with forget-me-nots.

Sleepwalking through the house,

I search for certificates

of authenticity—the gold seals

that could dispel this web that tangles

real and false, a new species

of fish, adapted to secrets and lies,

drifted up from a sea of raveling nets.

Then I discover whole new continents

of guilt inside

and forgiveness in a drop of rain,

but sleep is a mountain

I cannot climb.

No wonder

I wear a mask beneath a mask,

change signatures repeatedly,

and flamenco hips confuse

my red mud feet.

No wonder

my name shivers in a circle

of breath on glass, as I refuse

to choose a guide from

Mother knitting false halos

or Father polishing hooves,

both guarding the headwaters

that rise from two different worlds.

No wonder the mongrel dog's mouth foams

in my dreams when it hears drums

where sometimes it wants to burn and twirl

and other times fling itself over a waterfall.

No wonder I pick up feathers

and hear bones cracking

where I walk

behind the stars. I know

I am innocent but I know

where the burial grounds

are paved over for sunken treasure factories

and curio shops.

And I know that both the hand-tooled boots

and the beaded mules will carry my feet

to the owl's hideout

because we all dance on the same earth

that's pulling us in—

holding onto any molecules

of wonder we can find.

You Could Say

FOR MY FATHER

You could say

the man and his daughter have lost

their way and wandered through rain

on starless mesas, changed their names

so often the priest has fed their

confessions with cancelled prayers

into the paper shredder.

The man orders a wedge of cherry pie,

metal-flake red on Melmac,

she orders chamomile tea, settles

for Red Rose, and they both settle

into uneasy eye-to-eye and Naugahyde,

then fish for words, any words

to shore up the booth, sinking fast

into amnesia of rewritten histories

and wisps of truths that sneak up

from an ashtray in the non-smoking section,

but the words they were promised disappear

into foam, and they drag up

limp, weedy ones like Grandpa's suspenders

(his belt stays submerged

with the beatings, cigars

for cutting baby teeth, and the deaf-mute

saint with the hat from Saks

whose candles couldn't save him).

Then silence closes over them, silvery

and cold as plate glass

reflecting a two-tone Mercury

parked in purple smog of Handicapped—

he remembers the beaut he sold

for a song before the war

this time, enlisted; he'd die

or fight the rest of his life.

You could say

it was the end of the world

or D-Day, bombers launched

with the paint still wet, naked

blondes who led surprise attacks,

pulling on silk hose over the Atlantic,

silver rivets for nipples.

She tries to see him young and ready to die,

but his cowboy boots and bolo ties

can't bring back his smooth acolyte's

face. While he goes to "bring the car

around," she wonders if bigamists sleep well

or if their dreams split

in two, with two families of moons

orbiting the teeth they float

on the nightstand, snapping at stars.

He toots the American-made horn,

throws her his keys, and limps

to the passenger side, then it's *watch out*

for that dog, take a left there,

don't let that bastard horn in . . .

dammit shoulda taken Mowry. Arms descend,

bells clang, and he leans back, latticed

and lulled by train shadows,

lights flashing like frames

of an old, silent movie,

with moving mouths that don't match

the words and once-familiar names

scrolling past like scratchy credits

or headstone names that even he can't change.

You could say late-evening fog

rolling in from the bay lifts like a wing,

and he has a moment so lucid and pure

that he takes a newborn's breath, confessing

everything, and the daughter sees how it is

finally, understands, and gives

him a penance not just to confess

his sins but to name

what they are, and they could all go

home with the conductor's blessing,

and that bank of cumulus could part

overhead, absolving the stars,

connecting the dots between the old

and the yet-unnamed constellations.

Nothing Para Nada

This is a poem about nothing—
the nothing there is
living outside the stats,
accepting nothing and asking
nothing in return—the nothing
that circles in a déjà vu
holding pattern, waiting orders
from the tower that never come,
waiting to land
on a chromosome to begin
to be.
Even zeros are something—
circles of smoke
looping toward the new invisible
moon. Knowledge of an absence
is still knowledge, contained
by some bleached skull somewhere,
beholding.
Nothing, you would be a half-sister
twice removed, imagination's
cancelled check, if you would be
anything. But you, nothing,
are left blank in boxes
of ethnicity other no ones
refused to check.

Keep away mermaids, metronomes,

chandeliers, and pointed ghosts.

Keep away sombreros, sushi,

and hybrid corn.

Come here little invisible

playmate of invented borders

because all you have

is what others see,

and they only see what

you can believe in yourself.

Frost

Now...

Winter hard upon us,

windshields crusty with ice,

citrus growers calling out wind and fire

to save their oranges

from nature's holocaust.

With sharp sticks, we crack

the waxy crust of water pocketed

along the riverbanks.

Then...

You could smell the cold—

biting into your soul,

icy winds passed over granite

wings and shepherd's staffs

crooked around the frozen letters

of a long-untended name.

The moon, a sickle of light,

hid behind the owl's breath,

crystallized like hard, white

pellets in the air

as three women slept with hearth-

warmed stones, ears strained

separately for the same man's

return. But only the dirge

of a solitary train fell

out of the night, and once again he

slipped through the cracks in their dreams.

Even the train's call is colder

tonight, the tracks, two long

icicles melting into mist and darkness.

In the mountains, he gazed down

at green quilted with black and then up

at the undeniable truth of the sky.

With each breath, he took in a vastness

that would bring him as close

to heaven as he had ever hoped for.

How many times, he wondered,

could a man confess the same sin, laying

odds on the Almighty's memory lapse?

How many times could he outrun

the owl's call, the cold hook

of all the virgins' eyes

or the frond of the Bishop's crosier

curled around his neck

in dreams he'd wake from, soaked

with nighthawk chills and children's

voices bleating like lambs

lost in the frozen Milky Way?

I keep dreaming of snow,

a place in the mountains, familiar

yet beautifully strange.

Each night there are different journeys

to the same place and different

means of losing my way.

So many milky paths, so many

switchbacks.

How many ways are there to break

the spine of a dusty book where names

are webbed thin and undeniable—

but for a ghost trace left

on the just-erased slate? How many

names for the fatherless?

How many empty spaces in the heart,

in the blank pages of the soul?

This is what happened.

They had followed the trail of stars,

familiar to their footsteps,

the stars swollen as large

as they could remember,

pushing the herd higher up

toward greasewood and sage

on the sunny side of the butte,

led by the scrape and bong

of pebbles in rusty cans.

At first, the skies filled with flurries

soft as jackrabbit chins.

Then the winds darkened and howled

out of furious northerly mouths

across Missing Tooth Hill, up from

the arroyos. When the dog's eyes

foamed and he refused to budge,

the father tasted metal but still

followed a shearling, flower

of the flock, who had spooked and run.

They said lambs born in the dead

of winter were healthier, more adaptable.

When he turned again, the sky had

ruptured white and crashed around him.

He opened his mouth to call

for Pedro and swallowed an untamed

swirl between. Shreds of words

caught in his throat as he climbed

a ladder of white, not sure

whether he went up or down.

I wake on the eighteenth floor,

the city's bright roar hushed

and still under a weight

of whiteness that sweeps down

from another world; flakes large

as dimes spin and whirl.

In the dizziness of this white

pantomime, long-distance lines

crackle across the continent

as the phone just keeps ringing

like a cartoon phone dancing

in an empty room. Hours before,

she had already tipped the vial

into her mouth, then lay down

to wait, except for a slight tickle

in her ears, giving in to a numbness

that had been coming on for years.

The hours piled up like sheared

fleece and came to nothing

but the faint tickle of a distant

concertina in his ears.

They had stopped calling

for each other, conserving

breath like rationed candle wisps.

The pear tree blossomed and lifted,

hovering over the rickety gate

he must remember to mend;

the wind changed, and a covey

of white doves sprayed upward—

names offered like coins

from a big shot's pocket.

The father opened his mouth

one last time and let

flakes, brittle as communion wafers,

melt on his tongue, felt

them burn and disappear.

Spring, and frost still lies

like fleece on the ground. My tía

is fixing a hankie on my head,

explaining why I can't confess—

not one of the flock. Shifting

a dime from hand to hand in the backseat

of her Plymouth, I try to imagine the vat

of fire she is so sure of,

but all I can see are the lights

of oncoming cars growing larger and colder.

Pedro dug a hole under the snow,

closed his eyes, and conjured

rows of bush beans, serranos,

a halo of bacon-fat smoke

as he pulled himself tighter and tighter

into a knot, shrinking into

flickers of heat and promises

to the unmade bed of his future

where a woman slept, curled around

her own slumber and a dream, small

as a particle of light.

The howling had become one long

vowel, like a conch's pink lip

pressed to an ear, a softness nested

in the middle he would rise from.

My feet are cold as newly dug potatoes

lodged in frozen ground for centuries.

We heat bean-filled socks

in the microwave to warm our feet against

the sheets, cold as river rock

high in the Sierras. I spoon my body

against yours and re-run the film

of my former life as a child when

I took my sled out all day in the warm-cold

popsicle sun—still taste the stiff

wool of frozen mittens and hear the slice

of waxed runners in the packed snow,

bread wrappers inside galoshes snapped

over nylon snowsuits.

In a stillness so pure

it could ping, he opened his eyes,

wondering which world he was laid

out in and how could he stand

and go forth without hands or feet,

cold stumps bitten off at the cuffs,

how to plant seeds in frozen mud . . .

how to thaw and re-enter the spring?

Later, I come dragging the sled home

under a canopy of pine and beech snagged

with hard flakes of stars. That moment,

like any other but never forgotten—

that moment, so cold and bright,

when something vast opens out

of the embers and trembles into life.

She rubs her hands, dry and stiff

from the cold, the green of her eyes

so much like mine ... and theirs,

glistening with mica-like flecks

of fire in the river. A gutted stump

parts our path as we follow light

woven through bare saplings darkly

overlapping the riverbank.

Something white and feathery like milkweed

eddies in the air, snags in our hair—

something traveled miles and years

to arrive, to remind this world

of the other, these eyes ... of the others,

these stiff hands of the others ...

a reminder beyond the truth

of surfaces packed hard with ice—

the warning of another cold spell—always

ready to hold us if we hold each other

through the undeniable confluence

of blood and knowing and how

they matter to each other . . . let's tell

the truth . . . for once . . . both the names carved

in granite and the ones in melting ice.

IN MEMORY OF JOSE DEMETRIO DE JESUS SALAZAR, D. 1906 IN A

SNOWSTORM, AND HIS *OTHER* FAMILY LEFT BEHIND.

DANCING WITH THE SKELETONS

What does it take to live

in a world of invisible bones . . . to dance

when the only music

is the rattle of locks

that have lost their keys

or false teeth swallowing

what's written between the lines?

How many lies can a scaffold

of years support

before the cracks appear?

When spring thaws release

swallows and sap,

and winter's rigor mortis slackens—

whole villages of crypts and stones

can rise as the rivers give up spinners,

broken weathervanes, and bones

in a gush of rusty release—

so many clavicles, femurs,

scapulas clacking like

an old man's cane on the ice.

Up from a dark and dusty crevice,

you drag a box of photos: oil-stained

edges; windows of ragged, stair-

step children; sepia-spotted donkey carts;

rouged ladies with foamy hats;

and solemn girls in white veils, pale

as the missal that launched their path-

way to grace.

Who is the pretty one in polka dots?

Who tied the droopy bow

of the accordion-dwarfed girl

with the crimped edge of a familiar smile?

You stare and stare, knowing those patches

of shadows like your own.

You know as much as any children

who listen between the lines of Spanish

and English innuendos,

who learn to translate the secret

weather of their mother's colorless eyes.

But you never knew

just how much you really knew.

"These are your primos," they said. Together

you circled mulberry bushes

and farmers in dells, holding hands

in a ring of blood,

closed tighter than you knew.

Years later you'd say, "We knew,

but nothing we could have told."

You think you know the cost of naming,

of opening the book of bones—

dropping the needle down

to the old songs of call and response—

names floating through the violet cold

then dropped over a fence and gone—

playmates and primos who roam

neighborhoods and vacant lots

coming home to empty

plates and a sapling of rare switches

from which you're invited to pick your own.

But you don't know . . .

You don't know

the history of what she held

in, the running tab of indulgence,

of cold percale striped by tears of the moon.

Some things never add up . . .

matemáticas del corazón—no comprendo.

And you may not know

the double meaning of dear

in the days of rigid tintype,

the couple posed on horsehair and scrolled

oak, held together in an unbroken spell

of glazed vision and obligation.

Hard to imagine them holding each other

breast to breast in candlelight,

moving as one on polished parquet,

his feet and hers toe-to-toe, moving

in tandem—and harder still

to imagine how they did it—

later . . . and later . . . again, how she opened

to his need, hers crushed

with the rosary in another curled up

fist. Later, the clack of her beads

asking forgiveness—for whom?—

for the father?

for the wayward sprouts? the primos?

perhaps—for herself?

for the lies?—the family secrets,

family collusions? A concertina tinks

in the mist of distance—

the double-cross paso doble

they all mastered and passed on.

DAVY CROCKETT MEETS CORONADO

(RELATIVES WHO RESEARCHED GENEALOGY CLAIM WE ARE

RELATED TO BOTH.)

Whiff of pot liquor

and stewed coon hocks

smack into a bank of mussels y caracoles

drifting up from the gulf,

leapfrogging centuries

as Davy Crockett meets Coronado—

must be Tennessee,

those explorers veering off course again,

searching for spices, fountains,

and eternal stuff but finding cold scat,

chiggers, and forbidden real estate.

They give their names anyway

to peninsulas and sites

of future theme parks.

This day when they meet,

the air sizzles with polarities

sharp enough to be almost visible—

Coronado's compass twirls inside out,

and he is up to his shins in mud

the color of chile colorado.

Davy has sleepwalked for days

trying to dislodge from his head

a tune bounced

off a mountaintop, careened

from a coil of cotton baling wire,

zinged out of the future

from the mouth of a woman named Ella,

known for a kind of scat

Davy could never divine

that would send him up an unmarked trail

to the future parking lot,

where Fess Parker would flip

the keys of his classic Jaguar

to the classic black valet,

who will notify security

that a dirty old guy in buckskin

is digging up the asphalt,

armed and certainly dangerous, refusing

directions, as all men do.

Coronado had his chance

but hid from the women on spotted ponies,

preferring the alchemy of sunspots

and male intuition, which has now

brought them together; Davy,

humming like a bear in a winter trance;

Francisco, dragging his feathers

and heavy coat of mail

from one mirage to the next.

And so they meet—

dream walking, dyslexic warriors,

Coronado's parrot translating:

"That's some elegantiferous hat.

You new to these parts? Ya lost?"

Davy flashes a vote-getting grin.

"Don Francisco de Coronado lost? Two straits

I discovered yesterday, three corridors,

a small continent, and an isthmus.

You insult me, Señor."

"Don't go gettin' yer tail in a knot.

Somewhat of a scout myself.

Just took me two possums and a covey of quail

with one shot. I got the prettiest sister,

fastest horse, and ugliest dog. My father can whip

any man in Kentucky, and I can lick my father.

Sure you wanna go thataway?" Davy points

with Old Betsy. "There's Creeks up ahead."

"Sí, agua."

Davy grins, sun sparks on steel

as they take two steps apart—

a crooked Tennessee waltz bent for one second

into Flamenco Puro.

Then they turn and march

toward equidistant horizons and fates.

But Davy turns and hollers back

over a fringe of sweet gum,

"Y'all can go to hell . . .

Ahm going to Texas,"

which the ancient parrot translates:

"Thank you, Don Coronado, for the directions.

You have a lovely parrot."

CORNBREAD Y CARACOLES EN CIELO

FOR GRANDMA WINNIE AND GRANDMA DELUVINA

The grandmothers have been cooking

for decades now, preparing

la fiesta última, a supper

to last through eternity,

blending herbs and spices

from two worlds,

a menu of clashing flavors—

buñuelitos y biscuits,

black-eyed peas and habas catalana.

They will disagree, of course,

over how long to simmer the salsas,

how many pinches of filé or saffron,

whether to slice, chop, or mince

the garlic, the proper method

of steaming the rice . . .

braised rabbit or conejo con piñones.

On some things they'll never agree—

mayonnaise versus aioli,

bacon or unto to garnish,

and some of this bickering

will go on para siglos,

with sidelong glances, raised

eyebrows, little digs infantes—

"no sabes ni papa de concinar"—

with a spidery smile.

But the sounds

from the kitchen can be

a kind of music—

the thump of dough on floured

boards, the measured grinding

of garlic under a pestle,

wooden spoons slapping the sides

of bowls—the melting together

of dos mundos, the bitter limones

and the sweet, thick molasses,

the Tennessee waltz of Flamenco Puro—

rhythmical smells that cross

and harmonize the senses.

BLUE WALTZ PERFUME

FOR AUNT VICKIE-VICTORIA ASUSENA SALAZAR,

D. FEB. 13, 1956

Even in a greasy wind it lingers

on the pulse points of midnight,

a summer night in 1932.

If rain drips from the firs, it only

serves to sharpen the mock orange

sweetness that touches her earlobes

and brushes the blue-black nape

of her neck.

Returning from mass, her feet

discover a melody inside,

and she dances home, lifting her wrists,

circled with music, dancing past

a sycamore's heart-scraped names:

Victoria plus Tom—hers

will never heal, his scab

over like all the dull years

that follow—rooms of cold double

beds after she shuts the door

on his sloppy salud and Isle of Skye

denials. She'll take their girls,

sharpen her barber's scissors,

hang her ring in the bird's cage,

and laugh like crazy—teach

him to say, "Gimme a kiss Ricky."

"I don't care,"

and to kiss her on the lips.

I wanted to take you with me

to her bedside where she

is still young and blooming,

where her daughters twist rosaries

into wet knots of sorrow,

where shadows swallow her second

husband, so much younger

and not able to protest

the annulment that will allow

her last rites . . .

but that's not what I want to save.

I'll save the flight of her rippled fingers,

the old songs she played

by ear, Ricky scolding

the latticed light that combed

her shoulders, and how she could fall

into a waltz like a trance,

and if we close our eyes

time won't get in

our way, and if we breathe

in hard enough, the rusty hasp

of a box might release a scent

in 3/4 time—

a brief flood of Blue Waltz

breath the shadows have held

all these years.

ODE TO MY IMAGINARY SISTER

who sings "No Regrets" in Spanish,

dances on top of the stove

hot as a summer steering wheel,

full of piss and sunlight,

works at nothing

so much as her own desires—

belches at the symphony—

the violins at the peak

of crescendo—no apologies.

She twirls a string of nectar

and reflected light dripping

down to her bare toes,

sucks mangos at intermission,

juice shimmies down her chin

into a spangled navel—

"Vámonos, novia," she says,

"find a juke joint,

some hot blues and cold beers;

let's ride the stars bare-

back and blow your inheritance

on drinks para la casa."

You Were There

IN MEMORY OF HILDA FAY, THE HALF-SISTER I NEVER KNEW

You were there
all along—
you were the room we never opened,
the song no one remembered the words
to—other half of my loneliness,
the detour he took and then denied.

In a three-ring blow-up pool I skim
the bottom, eyes open, swim through rings
of my own breath, seeking a new route
into the haunted heart.

What to do with a sister unveiled
thirty years later by telephone?
Mother's vengeance no doubt—a secret
sister—must be put away like the Madam
Alexander doll with perfect curls
no one was allowed to even touch.

But you were there all along, faded
square in the photo album—packed in
tight with peony buds cracked open

in a hushed deflowering. A page

of crippled fractions—I'm learning to

subtract and divide—to take away

and to carry—but none of this helps

to fill the hole—he is the maestro.

The new-book smell chokes me. You are the one

divided—a shadow equation

with no sum, the square root of loss—he

taught us long division and no way to

save the remainders.

A letter waits unclaimed—hovers in

a postal holding pattern, filed

in the dead-letter slot—as if asleep.

With covers over her head, she sleeps

far away in patent-leather shoes.

She dreams of boats and trains in sets of

two. He sleeps in his own holding pattern

and dreams also of trains—steaming backward

and lost luggage because the map of

his heart is folded and creased from his

journeys—because he was always set

to leave at a moment's notice, and

he knew he could because of his gift

for magical history.

A U-Haul passes in green smoke of

the dinner hour. I curl my toes hard

into the hooked rug, lock fists around

arm rests, holding on as if all this

could rise in a blink, hover, and then

touch down in Idaho—time to make

a new life—time to use the new name,

time to trade Green Stamps for that double

bypass, the one where your heart is pulled

out and flipped like a coin directing

us north, south, anywhere away from

that hollow draining.

You were the sister I wanted to

fight with, to call into jump rope

songs, to touch the sky with, to wash the

spiders off—Shabushka, Shabushka,

Shabushka. But cypress, spruce, and larch

scrape the wind between us, reach higher

into the distance, spearing the dust

that holds us apart.

Now we are two boats navigating

with memorized charts, birds pulling us

in separate directions—one builds

a mute nest of bone and twigs, soft as

gauze. The other sings invisible

notes and weaves them in the center of

spiky thorns. Because we were halved, the

moon waned between us, the tides pulled us,

boats lapping ever farther apart.

On the crippled Greyhound, an old man

shook his cane at smog, Taco Bell, and

Reagan, that son of a bitch. He no

longer had any use for his skin,

so he bandaged it in Rainbow bread

bags and let his eyes roll inward. Legs

wrapped in tight strips of elastic, she

emptied pans of yellow piss and coils

of shit, flicked his arm for a good vein.

When morning light blinked through the transom,

she slid the needle in clean and sweet—

sang to herself on the bus, a song

we'd never share. Then she played the old

game, searching men's faces for familiar

shadow planes, just as I searched faces

for hers, played nurse without knowing why.

Strapped down to a gurney, I'm in no

position to argue when they stab

into my spine and half of me drifts

away—like a boat cut in two—

unmoored, only to dock later,

gutted and swept clean of the mass that

had stopped dividing—had spun out of orbit.

One man between two women stands on a

platform, one at each end. From far off

a train shrills. Each wears a hat of feathers

from different birds, both endangered species.

One looks down at the tracks, the other

looks up into clouds of migrating

moths. Their perfumes seep out and mingle

in a storm of peppery rose and

moss magnolia, two scents that collide

and wing off into railway fumes.

Taking down the box of photos, I

lay them out like a fortune-teller—

shuffle and reshuffle the faces

until I find my own eyes—only

darker—and the bent corners of my

mouth—only older—and hold the photo awhile

like a scapular or a rosary

death card—a child who both knows and doesn't
know what it means. Outside, snow falls, a
car door slams, and a phone rings and rings
in a distance I'll spend my whole life
crossing. One day in a new life the
letter will finally arrive, and
when the phone rings, I'll answer, but the
voice at the end of the line will be
another man's, a stranger's who will
tell what I've always known, that you were
there all along. But then it will be
too late.

Summer's bounty—a friend brings tomatoes,
apricots from Mother's tree, our dentist
gives us fish. The crapes bloom and scatter
purple curls. With so much bounty, surely
we could fill ourselves, surely we could
fill this hunger that self sustains. On
blue coils of exhaled air, I float face
down in the pool—full of emptiness,
sharp and sweet because loss can be hugged
close when it's all that you are given,
and absent memories can hold you
afloat when there is nothing else below.

The Recipe

FOR MY GRANDDAUGHTER HEATHER AND MY MOTHER

is familiar, a blend

of clabbered milk and something wounded,

one cup bitter almond,

hard sauce brought to the boiling point,

a pan of gray drippings

thrown to the curdled skies

where a girl in her late teens

stares down from a broken bridge

into her own muddy reflected eyes.

Pot roast lingers long past

twilight's chill

as something stalls inside,

like her father's Model T

hiked up on blocks in the weeds.

Nothing changes in the sad

museum of discontent.

Now she looks out a window

where two girls in Barbie pink

practice karate chops

and a neighbor kid smashes

Robo Cop against a minivan.

She wants to go up in flames,

to melt in the pot roast–Sunday air,

or at the very least

to congeal into another set of molecules,

but even the stripes she's

dug into her thighs

don't match up with the pain inside.

She is curled up in bed,

tired enough to let the truth

hover where it will,

tired enough to let go and turn

away from tobacco-stained men

galloping after foxes

on the mortgaged walls.

If she stays there,

refusing school, Bible verses,

buttermilk, and even chess pie,

they will only whisper in the hallway—

home remedies that saved no one.

And there are no fitful lights out yonder

to save her either,

no insurance premiums

not in arrears to cover this.

At best, a distant cousin

could take her in

for a month or two; so gradually

she'll rise and re-enter

the world of supper and sums.

But something's missing

and multiplying both—

there are more rooms and more

girls, and the moon comes and goes

in a spell of long division.

It hangs on a nail

in the pantry, beside an apron

mapped with jam and hard

sauce, the stains of various meals.

The smell of rancid leftovers

swims into the eaves, enters

the dreams of girls asleep

in pink and yellow rooms

decades apart. One dreams

of sad songs and measuring spoons

lost in the magnetic push

of opposing forces

and a storm of saffron from Spain.

The other sifts dry ingredients,

folds it all together

in a heavy bowl,

then forgets to light the fire.

But always there are tears

for salt and substitutions

for what they are lacking

and what they each must bear.

In the parallel museum of sorrows,

the aprons are perfectly displayed,

every discolored patch and blotch

bared to the hard light—

infinity effect of aprons stretching

from window to window

across the miles and years—

artifacts of all the secrets spilled

and kept—the shared

and well-preserved stains.

BEACH WALKING WITH THE STONES

FOR ZOË LUNA

"You can't always get what you want"

tumbles around in my head,

holding Zoë's hand,

combing the sand for fallen bits

of the moon. What more could I want?

She's two, and everything is hers:

the surf, sandpipers, ropy piles of seaweed,

billions of toy pebbles, polished

just for her.

A man plastered with Nike

stops and offers two sand dollars.

I smile, but his face tells me

they are offered only for admiration

or envy. "They're perfect," I say

just as Zoë reaches for them.

Tugging her away,

"You can't always get what you want,"

I say. "Look baby, don't touch."

Fingers extended, her face crumbles,

then falls to the bottom of the sea.

"But if you try sometime . . ."

"Keep looking, keep looking," he throws

over his shoulder, dancing away

as if we must be looking

for what he's looking for.

"Moonstones," I sing, "we want moonstones,

you dolt," offering one, white

as frozen milk, to the hand reaching

up to mine, ". . . you get what you need."

Yes, he's given us just

what we need, a stolen

glimpse inside—to guard against

where our own envy, avarice, greed

burrows like a mindless sand crab.

And now I give it back to you.

PART II

OUTSIDE

CAYUCOS FOG

Beyond the dark rail, nothing

drops off into nothing

but trust, all the grand

words gone in vast sheets

of whiteness, like invisible ink.

White rabbits morph into cumulus

top hats that collapse into scarves

of dizziness, where the horizon

smokes and turns away

into dreams of sleep, rocked

to sea slap and flap of wind sock

and towels, prayer flags to everyday

icons and the ordinary ho-hum

splendor of the sea.

ODE TO A BOY AT THE BEACH

as dark as his shadow

scattering white gulls,

nudging against the tide.

Toes nibble the edges of foam

as he works his way into the surf.

Twisting, his shadow gleams

like burnt driftwood on wet sand.

He's come to the edge of a continent

to dip into the unknown,

to test himself against the roar

from deep within the sea, the undertow

of history, the great white

shark, the soundless knock of ancestors'

bones lining the bottom of the sea.

AMERICA'S MOST WANTED

8—

He wanted them—

the bruises so easily hid

by long sleeves and Levi's

on his sister's sparrow limbs—

but settled for stuffing guilt

in a pillow with his fist

to "Knock some sense" into it

and stockpiled cotton from aspirin jars

to jam in his ears

at night when Uncle Jack bowled

with empty Coors bottles

down the hall.

But the TV in his head

broadcast live all night—Candelaria's

face, mute and splotched as the moon.

12—

"They don't want

half-black and Mexican boy children,"

the social worker said, shuffling his papers

to the bottom of the heap.

But the couple in the Camry wanted her;
they would take the sister, the lady
already lapping her hair into thick braids.

All he wanted
was that squishy flap flap
when he replaced baseball cards
with pollywogs in bicycle spokes.
And he wanted his parents'
snake-tongued arms,
inky devils with hard-ons,
wrapped around him even as the waterline
of hatred rose in his heart,
and moonspill fell on Iron Man
sheets soaked with pee.

18—
Monica spit his ring out, said
he'd flunked two blood tests,
she was through.
The hammer in his heart smashed
what was left,
cruisin' Kings Canyon with Lil' Player
crooning, "I want you, I need you,
and I love you," firing rounds
at the bus depot ladies' room.

28—

Have you seen me?

says the carton he tips

upward to drain behind the dumpster

in back of Chow Fun's,

where his name rumbles nearby on TV.

       She'd wanted a fix,

          left him with a maid at Motel 6 after

          she delivered on a garbage bag.

       It wasn't that

          she didn't want him,

          it was just that helium fog,

          stepping off the ledge into

          nothing that she wanted more.

And now he's wanted

nationwide, his face, dark

as a bruise on syndicated TV

news, where they re-enact his crimes—

the ones he's finally wanted

for—the ones Candelaria's new mother

will erase with one quick flip

of the remote.

CONDUCTOR'S LAMENT

Rain spills against gazebos

and rows of stone Marys sucked

into gravity's Easter basket. Nothing

is safe it seems. They are stealing

trees again, baby figs and orange

saplings still wet beneath the buds.

They are losing children again, handing

them over to strangers in bus depots,

turning backs on toddlers beside

railroad tracks where altars of tear-

shaped bouquets and thrift-store teddy bears

will appear with ghosts full of grace

and what looks like the blood of broken

thermometers, a wet shine pearling the rails.

ART LESSON WITH THE HEARING-IMPAIRED

Imagination is more important than knowledge. —Einstein

I'm here with paints and brushes,
coffee cans of water, the stuff
they can hold and reach with
beyond their muffled borders,
metal and glass—the frames of
their hard-won, objectified land,
safe with the dangerous edges.

Perched on the chair back
like a dark crow,
Tony draws a graveyard,
signs that they all died
in a freeway crash, executes
a wounded swan dive, smacking the floor
with his flimsy chest.

Billy's Popeye arms lift the school
over his head. Thin, birdy fingers
grip a green crayon he's colored
all his nails with and his chin.

The plugged holes where Michu's

ears should be are infected

and draining again. He's under

the desk, lost in purple,

soundless scribbles, a fence

where he's safely corralled.

Celine draws a house of glass

windows and no doors, no way in

or out, just a peek through crossbars

where all is sleep tight and orderly,

and no monkey curtsies

for the queen of what could be.

Here there are no karaoke kangaroos

or laughing shoes. Here are only

sharp-cornered dreams that bruise

and freeway pileups of hard-edged nouns.

Then Rindy draws a princess

with lopsided crown, diamonds

big as plums, leaves off

her glasses, draws big, lashy

blue eyes and silver-crayoned moons

in place of hearing aids.

Unrealistic body image, the teacher says,

but I pretend I can't hear—

take a large sheet of paper

that shines with water and paint—

a castle, I say, for anyone

who wants to come, free bluebird

flights this week only.

Slowly, Celine paints a door,

then as the sun slides from behind

a cloud, the room slowly fills

with light and she steps

over the threshold into nothing—

moves her hands in strange, frilly

signs no one has ever seen before.

SMOKE SIGNALS

Above the honk and shine of chrome

on a slow-spinning Shell sign

a brown sparrow perches, lost

in reverse orbit, blessed by four

stations of the wind, at home

blended with motion and sky, watched

by a larger-than-life-size eye

circling White Rose Optical.

Caught in a tunnel of light

from above, a carload of Crip boys

wave hands like flags of lands unknown

to them, signals from lost tribes

flapping toward the eye in the sky,

birds cut off from their wings.

Pruning Roses at Corcoran Prison

for George Moats

Through black, wiry arm hairs

inky roses trail, wrapped

around a fat bicep, unwinding

a scroll of Rubaiyats,

Perpetuals, Climbing Night.

On C yard he smells

electrical perfumes,

snips the tired blooms back

to leaves spread like five fingers.

He knows the bite of White

Knight, Lowell Thomas, Queen

Elizabeth, knows what they can do

to him; his hands have learned

directly from teeth

buried under the soft skirts.

The Nam vet who heads the garden crew

has taught him what to do—

how to leave the center clean,

removing scaled and lesioned

limbs, sacrificing

old wood for new.

Taking one bloom for another,

sour chow-breath blends with

sweet when he bows to them,

much like his brother's kowtow

to American Beauty, Camelot,

Chrysler Imperial, Oklahoma—

memory's thorn of love

blooming inside a dark thigh,

creeping up a ropy neck,

spiky, anonymous valentine art,

always the same generic dream—

a past or future country

where it's not always lockdown,

not always the dormant season.

VIRGIN BEHIND SECURITY BARS

Only jasmine, chorizo, and suicide prayers

sift through these locked bars

that would ruffle the wings

of a weaker saint. Still, I have no way

to leave or enter the night.

From my cage of netting and electric

lights, I watch the parade to Joy's

Liquor King, with elephants, angels,

aloe vera, and American flags for comfort,

and black-widow eggs rolled softly

into the nape of my neck.

Sometimes a falling star twines

with a cry from childhood, circling

back to its beginning; a song

escapes from a cracked headstone

and finds me standing here, stalled

like a broken-down circus

on the freeway. But sometimes objects

that may appear smaller in side-view

mirrors really are smaller

and swerve into the moon's blind spot—

saving a family of six;

sometimes a bomb doesn't go off,

a cancer cell refuses

to divide, and someone

opens the tracks of their arms—

palms upward to the Milky Way.

These are the miracles no one sees,

immovable objects that collide—

the moon growling at a three-legged dog,

the wind gathering petitions

even of the faithless, who don't ask

favors, don't ask

if I can grace their dashboards

or tilt their wheels into the spin

when it comes, which is the real test—

the only one that matters.

KILLDEER

FOR THE WOMEN AT VALLEY STATE PRISON, CHOWCHILLA

The killdeer is by most people called "a noisy bird and restless ... because men and dogs are ever in pursuit of the poor thing[s]." If you cannot find pity for the poor birds ... you take up their eggs and see their distress; but if you be at all so tender-hearted as I would wish you to be, it will be quite unnecessary for me to recommend mercy! —James J. Audubon

1. Janeen
"Killdeer," says the blonde, blue-eyed
ex-Marine lifer pointing across the yard.
She still surrenders
to her man's cold, sculpted arms
in sleep, where he's rearranging
the constellations, leaving marks
with beautiful names—abrasions,
lesions, plum and gamboge
contusions hidden under her dress
uniform with bold stripes. Bones,
unlike secrets, mend quietly as sleep
where the killdeer call to her—
their cries, luxuries
she still denies herself.

2. Cookie

"Here's the fat bitch wanting

her insulin," the guard sings

as if his secrets aren't known

to her, aren't grist

for the girls in the mix,

his private dancers who strip

and rearrange his shadows for

early unlocks. She whispers

her secrets to the killdeer,

who carry them outside like heavy love

letters laced with germs.

3. Mary Sad Heart

A wash of eerie maize light

bathes the emptying yard

and the one with a birthmark

of Venus and the moon

on her sole. Only the killdeer

cry for her, screeching into stars

that taunt like sparks of ancient Tule fires—

a cindery touch that burns inside

and out, leaving only the faintest

light dimming from the Elder's

denying eyes, leaving her with secrets

heavy as obsidian.

4. Venus

When yard recall leaves only

the buzz of halogen and a school

yard's ringing after-hush,

killdeer hop from razor wire

into pools of sprinklered light,

picking at the leftovers

of tobacco and smuggled dinner rolls,

and when they cry into the unfenced

stars that glimmer as far away

as dreams deferred, their cries

echo what's lost inside—

bits of swallowed secrets

and promises—justice

later, that never comes—only

stray crumbs left behind, dropped

in mud and Venus's afterglow.

STELLAR JAY SONNET

FOR CATHERINE AND CASCADELL

Night is at the door, asking

to join us again, its voice

weak and thin as veins

of light that gradually reveal

a dark stain under the table,

all the shine squeezed out

of a body no larger

than a tube of paint—all its indigo

spattered away—all its purple song

smashed flat as hardened pigment.

The unfilled wings—flat, lost kernels

of sound—rub up against this new

darkness, this new shade of black

that opens like a mouth, accepting.

THE PARROT AT EMERALD THRIFT

In the midst of stringless violins

and broken princess phones,

a garbled vowel punctuates

the swamp-cooled aisles of Emerald Thrift.

It's the only freedom left

to him: anomalous, guttural repetitions

of a wizened child performing for pistachios.

But the child tugging her mother's skirt

does not mistake its cry for one of her own,

just watches, eyes wide and wild

as the bright feathers open

and ask her name

in a voice clearly out of place.

He mocks her mother's cell phone voice—

"Brrrrrack! Lincoln's Birthday sale!"

Shackled to peeling French provincial,

he bows to a mock sun, ambassador of lost

green rivers and pink half-off tags,

indentured to bald mannequins and old men

shuffling by in carpet slippers

keeping time to false teeth that clack

down the pocket hole of memory,

a call for parrots and baby dolls

whose stolen voices cry for no one—

not even themselves or the tarnished fingers

of Asian children threading wings

of gnats to stitch the ears of hibernating

teddy bears. Who split the lark to find

the music? Who marked down the tone-deaf

mermaid, rolled back the price of syllables?

Didn't anyone tell you that there's now

a market in the new global economy

for bilingual larynxes and outsourced

diphthongs—that the voices

of your children's children

are caged and ready for shipping?

WATCHING THE WIZARD OF OZ ON SPANISH TV

Charged with his safekeeping

while they are in the fields, Rosa

is to make sure that nothing makes him cry.

So when Dorothy's house flaps up

into the sky, she pats Tomás and says,

"No that can't happen to us."

But when the tornado eats even the dog,

she remembers the crossing—

how the dust devil's angry skirts

twirled around them, how they tasted

its red fury for hours, how they dug dirt

from their ears and nose and scalp for days.

Tomás is crying, so she wraps herself

around him like a warm serape, clucks,

"No preocupes, mijo," as the Wicked Witch

of the West wags her finger, vowing vengeance.

But Rosa knows tonight she'll dream

again of the desert, covering her head

to hide from falling stars and helicopters—

no red slippers

to keep her safe, just crumbling Nikes

with new cardboard every day.

Now Tomás smiles as Dorothy dances

down yellow brick,

clicking her red heels . . .

"No hay ningún lugar como la casa"—

his face beaming turquoise TV light.

Back then, shoes skipped into Rosa's dreams,

new boots for treacherous gullies

and rock-cobbled paths, washed-out roads

that would lead her to cities paved with

Gringo dollars, America's Oz.

Her shoes were red then, caked with dirt

and darker red when the blisters burst.

They had walked around the earth twice,

not stopping for dust storms, rattlers,

or scorpions. They slept in foxholes and

scorched their eyelids in the sun.

Tomás is asking if there are Munchkins

for real. "You are a Munchkin,"

she says, tickling him into his bag.

We are Munchkins, she thinks, chased by

La Migra who can send us back to homes

no longer our homes. Tío Ramón disappeared

last week, taken in a raid at the truck stop,

and no one knows where he's gone

or if he has his meds. Monique's papi

was sent with her brother and two primos.

Monique's mamá hides her in a storage shed,

won't let her go to school.

Rosa flips off the TV as Dorothy fills

the screen with "El algún sitio sobre el arco iris . . .

las aves vuelan sobre el arco iris. ¿Por qué,

ah, por qué, verdad?" face shining with

saintly Hollywood light.

"Mira Rosa," Tomás calls, "I'm clicking mis pies . . .

No hay ningún lugar como la casa," he sings.

"No hay ningún lugar como la casa."

"No, not like that," Rosa frowns.

"There's no place like home . . .

there's no place like home . . . en Inglés, mijo.

¡En Inglés!"

OVERTIME AT THE
PAUL REVERE MOTEL

(MR. AND MRS. G.O. PATRIOT ON VACATION)

Fabreeze-laced, the satin spread

shimmies for a quarter;

purple TV lips sing

feminine hygiene tips.

They channel-surf from Connie Chung—

". . . in China, English is the number one language . . ."

"So what's up with the U.S.?" he says—

to rainbow hymns flickering

8:06 and 58 degrees—

to the latest immigration raid

on Kindergarten terrorists.

"Not a white in sight," he says,

bringing margaritas from the bar.

"Gonna run us outta this country,"

she replies, lifting her glass

to Van Gogh fishing boats

that hide stowaways in the hold

and invisible worms that gnaw the bamboo

headboard, grow fat on Welfare

and tips, multiplying in the plum-

harvested sunset, while the vertical

blinds repeat the gossip of

Ecuadorian maids to the moon

trapped in the parallel universe

of narco corridos and rap.

In the morning, they wake with salt-

rimmed lips to chattering maids

next door folding toilet paper

into triangles, square-cornering sheets.

Heading out for Egg McMuffins,

fat hamburger clouds sizzle on the horizon,

gathered cumulus of the working poor.

Later, the maid will find, left in a drawer,

a red-eyed Polaroid One-Step poodle,

four carats parked on its rhinestone collar

beside the Bush-Cheney bumper of an SUV—

four carats that dug in a purse

for a quarter tip left on the nightstand

beside the open Gideon Bible.

MUSCATEL SONNET

You follow the old man

who hauls a plastic garbage bag,

sloping up the street—

feel its drag and clank

tugging like ballast, a hard

pull backward that you must pull

against in order to drag

your sorrows along the path

of least resistance, scrap-metal feet

chugging toward all that can be

hoped for, a clear night

for Jupiter's blessing, a bag

of smashed cans too full for regret,

a warm spot in your gut.

3-D JESUS

(DOUBLE SONNET)

Fish jump through the sadness of sales tax,

as the transparent man whose wig

is darker than his beard stands with

hands open and raised, sandwiched

in Kodak rainbows, blind prophet

of our own blindness, paid less than

minimum, no benefits, caught

between Tampax machines, cinnamon

breath mints, and headlines of movie-

star adoptions and mercury

overdose. 3-D Jesus

walks on a waterfall, hands raised

as if to call his flock of lost

fishermen, pale as stock options.

A Miracle Vue Production,

made in Japan, land of micro-

miracles, fine-laminated

food, assembly-line Buddhas, and

conveyor belts of plastic, waterproof

saints, all landfill-proven immortal.

Spinning round on a drugstore rack,

his plastic, raining eyes will never

see the homeless woman exchanging

blood for Diet Coke. She can't afford

his redemption. Her only hope is what she spies

behind him on the shelf—infinity effect

of her own reflection—and what she'll slip

into the depths of her moonless pockets.

Fiber-Optic Angel

Who could want you? Poor

seraph with firecracker wings,

trailer-trash trinket, fallen

from heaven's mail order

of marked-down miracles.

Only a plastic sconce nailed

to faux oak paneling

could bear your light,

fan it upward to a heaven

of glitter-dusted acoustic.

Only an infomercial host

gossiping with Cher

could ever imagine you holy,

able to hark or herald

in Hamburger Helper fumes.

What could a tricked-out

glow-in-the-dark host

tell us about glory

or even suburban tremors?

But sometimes . . .

a dusty electron or two escapes

into a drop of Pledge

and Colt Forty-five, releasing

a golden strand of light that

pours through the fiberglass drapes

into the rabbit ears pricked

to stray celestial tunings

and limited-time offers of eternity.

Then lost Scrabble tiles

realign on the console TV,

silk flowers levitate, back-dropping

her wings of glass, thin as cricket

breath, and a hidden portal opens

so you can enter with nothing but her

subliminal blessing and a credit card.

Jesus Loves You at the Venus Beauty Salon—Fifth Avenue, Fresno

If the kid is there,

I'll tap my gritty quarters

on the glass display

of pink crullers

and tiny, frosted inner tubes

lined up at Jimmy's Doughnuts.

He'll pass me his day-old

smile, a maple bar, and overlook

the quarters once again.

Jesus Loves You,

but he just puts up with me,

I'll sing out the door, passing

the Sorry, We're Closed sign

of Open Door Ministries,

my face bobbing over flocks

of red, white, and blue angels

and choirs of geishas at Shooting

Star Gifts, on my way

to Venus Beauty Salon,

where I empty trash and sweep

up tumbleweeds of hair.

"I was married once," Venus says,

"to a doctor who gave himself shots

and drank his own pee;

didn't last though, maybe

he wasn't a doctor . . .

Fogged in shortwave, the second one

muttered in the cellar all night

with the door closed, big

plans he had to warn the Pentagon—

magnetic storms and secret codes

he broke, with the others like him.

Then there was Fred, big

on curly fries and short

on romance, born-again

to Bowling For Jesus.

Found the Lord myself a few times,"

Venus says, "but kept misplacing him . . ."

She pats her brown #5 waves

smooth as one of Jimmy's French twists

and winks out the jingly abierto door.

Hefting a King Cobra from A-1 Liquor,

Jimmy toasts the rows of security doors

where whiskey-sour blonde

tumbles with mushroom pearl. Brunette

Serenade rolls into unholy

alliance with Jimmy's greasy doilies,

smudged tithing pledges, and rusty

hangers from Fifth Avenue—

one giant strip-mall hairball.

"Business is picking up," he says,

offering Flaming Hot Cheetos

with a quick bump bump in his eyes.

I want to say that my guy has a big

rig or that I am taken, married

to a cloud in a ceremony attended

only by two sparrows and a broom.

I was given away by the sun, and my wild

cirrus lover does not clean toenails

with a steak knife, takes me

duro y slow, and does not spit

in parking lots. But instead, I say,

"Gracias, no," slide around the corner

past the balloon bouquets and Jesus

crucified on a palm tree shadowed

by the #28 bus, a blurry altar

of clouds and marked-down Marys.

Please God, abierto, abierto—

help the kid get through

the next round of treatments—let Venus

roll her horoscope into one more month

of quarters, abierto, no appointment needed—

as for me, no shooting stars, I can get by—

just a window of sultry clouds at night,

abierto, so they can slide over the sill

into my room, one small sign of grace,

por favor, the opposite of a miracle.

FIXED-INCOME SONNET

Take the dull edge of blue

from unsharpened knives

and smoke, whispering thin as fly's

wings trapped in the sill, a plume

noosing around the old man who's

rocking to dog snores and mating cries

of geese lifted to the dirty skies,

tarnishing like old copper baby shoes,

dark relics of the dreamy past when

peaches big as beach balls fell

out of the boughs, and the yolky sun

smelled of salt, pollen, and cinnamon.

Light trickles down from the rafters, never

enough to even read the latest budget cuts.

Yard Sale in the Fog

FOR LUIS OMAR SALINAS, D. MAY 2008

All the mad need is a ride somewhere. —*Omar Salinas*

Only those who've lost their shoes

could find the broken wheelchair.

Only those who've smelled time could stumble

upon the table of fermenting Avon

and outdated atlases

or strum the stringless ukulele.

With only cigarettes to spend, he stowed

away in a Magi-clean truck, hearing crickets

and cracked acoustics of the night

nurse charting under his breath.

Wearing a flannel robe and Burger King

crown, he cheeked his meds

and eloped in the fog, drawn toward

the sweet loneliness of "Fool on the Hill,"

the smell of Folgers and sugar glaze,

with no plan but to fly on the leftover

breath of starlings and blue

hydrangeas for as long as the sky

would have him.

And he palmed the broken Bic,

because no matter where he goes

he takes along the wounded spark

some also call madness.

With care, he collects

fluffy Day-Glo slippers, bent valentines,

and pillowcases embroidered

with someone else's tears,

the frayed provisions needed

for his borrowed journey.

DUSTY FOOTSTEPS

AFTER AND FOR BORGES

Today I have been thinking

beyond the rain

of yesterday and now, beyond

the weight of dusty thoughts, tatted

into threes, a rosary of air

ticking dirty–clean–dirty–clean.

I don't mind this shapeless body,

these ragged stumps—

I gave my feet away

to the crippled stars,

stumbled, and made a bargain

with dust.

Today I have not rotated

your mattress and beat it

free of mothy lust.

I have not rubbed all your black cups

white as bone nor polished

the dots from unrolled dice.

With feathers and fine steel

wool, I've tickled the eyes

of angels blind,

napped on the needles of tombstones,

watched spider breath

unravel morning on my grave.

Now let the moon bulge and shrink,

the second hand steal bread

from the orphanage of Thursday.

Vallejo has come and gone,

leaving his muddy boots

on the stoop, while footsteps

still echo from afar, and the hours

spill recklessly as rain

that falls where and when

it damn well pleases,

draws the sky and the earth

together in lazy connect-the-dots.

Today I have been thinking,

squandering thoughts, surely God will forgive

an old lady who forgets to brew his tea.

WHAT'S AMAZING ABOUT GRACE

(DOUBLE SONNET)

At the risk

of mocking the sermon on display

behind the mock lighthouse

of a church on Ocean Avenue,

surely you see

how it depends

on inflection,

modulations of a mind

behind the words—everyone's

talking about the power

these days, of words,

how there is nothing

beyond what

we invent ourselves.

Beneath the sign

in overlapping light

and shade of window slats,

a stray grackle

picks crumbs from among

the sparse offering of pebbles,

a flick of quicksilver black—hard

to imagine someone

choosing, perhaps

a creator saying, "That one

that black . . . no blue . . . no

there—just that touch

of fire, cobalt night

blended . . . now fly."

THE PULL

(DOUBLE SONNET)

The longer you sit in the dark,

the more you see

dark wings open slowly,

old scribbles return,

the moon pour through wisteria.

Mars spins, a worn, red top

on the night's playroom floor.

Moonlight slices the fence slats;

leaves scratch on cement,

faint plink on aluminum.

On the silver water's face,

a blow-up swan slides in circles,

thrill of the pull—the face

crayoned outside the shadow lines.

The one who lives in the bog

or under the trestle

reaches up for bare ankles,

leaps from embers

stirred from the charred place

where old fears gestate,

tugs at shirt-tail or hem,

pulls you toward its soft, dark

bin in the cellar, where you find

yourself, or part of

the past you thought buried,

the slug-softness where you fear nothing

but nothing; even with eyes closed

you'll still hear the sound of digging.

LONG AGO THE SAME

Winter

smoke enters the low clouds

pressing down on a bitter ridge of trees

on the hill

horses snort cold blue

bottle flies dance before death

swallows the first star

you wait and wait

but no one calls

your name—so familiar   this

trampled nest

this cracked song circling round

isn't this the same place

you thought you had left

long ago   the same

cold light twisting from shadows

across the broken cornfield

the same hungry train

sinking deeper and deeper

into darkness   that answers

the unspoken question

no one is there to answer

you're still afraid

to ask   watching silent

redwing blackbirds unfurl

flags whipping through circles

of icy breath you send

to lasso

the sweet amnesia

of long ago   and now   a different same.

ACKNOWLEDGMENTS

Arabesque, 2007: "America's Most Wanted"

Askew, 2006: "Subjunctive Mood"

Blue Arc West Anthology of California Poets, 2006: "Virgin Behind
    Security Bars"

Café Solo, 2006: "Cornbread y Caracoles en Cielo"

Café Solo, 2007: "Prison Roses" ("Pruning Roses at Corcoran Prison")

Future Cycle Magazine, 2008: "Fiber-optic Angel"

Homage to Vallejo, 2006: "Dusty Footsteps"

The Packinghouse Review, 2009: "No Wonder"

Rattle, 2005: "The Parrot at Emerald Thrift"

Snake Nation Review, 2006: "Blue Waltz Perfume"

So Luminous the Wildflowers, 2003: "Jesus Loves You at the Venus Beauty
    Salon—Fifth Avenue, Fresno"

Undercurrents, 2006: "Cayucos Fog"

U.S. Latino Review, 2000: "Davy Crockett Meets Coronado"

ABOUT THE AUTHOR

Dixie Salazar has published three books of poetry: *Hotel Fresno* by Blue Moon Press in 1988, *Reincarnation of the Commonplace* (National Poetry Book Award winner) by Salmon Run Press in 1999, and *Blood Mysteries* by the University of Arizona Press in 2003. *Limbo,* her novel, was published by White Pine Press in 1995. She has also published numerous poems and some short stories in about sixty different literary journals, including *The Missouri Review, The Red Brick Review, Poetry International,* and *Ploughshares,* as well as contributed to quite a few anthologies such as *Many Californias, Unsettling America,* and *Highway 99.*

Currently she teaches English at California State University and shows oil paintings and collage work at the Silva/Salazar studios at 654 Van Ness in Fresno, California. Her visual artwork has been shown in the Central Valley, San Francisco, Las Vegas, and New York. Her work can be viewed at www.dixiesalazar.com. She has also taught extensively in California prisons and the Fresno County jail.

A dual heritage inspires not only the poetry in her newest work but also much of her visual artwork. "Memories are an important part of the bridge of self-discovery, and I remember crossing the bridge, but sometimes I don't have clear memories of the scenery along the way. On one side was my father's world: Spanish speaking from las montañas. On the other side was my mother's world: a deep southern drawl wafting from the magnolia and chinaberry trees. Writing and visual artwork (connecting the past, present, and future and transcending all) has become the primary constant for me, a bridge to span the disparate worlds," Salazar has said. Identity issues are what drive most of her work in ongoing explorations.

Library of Congress Cataloging-in-Publication Data

Salazar, Dixie.
  Flamenco hips and red mud feet / Dixie Salazar.
    p. cm. -- (Camino del sol)
  ISBN 978-0-8165-2851-6 (pbk. : alk. paper)
  I. Title.
  PS3569.A459187F63 2010
  811'.54--dc22   2009029729

Breinigsville, PA USA
11 January 2010
230551BV00002BA/1/P